LETTER TO A FRIEND WITH THE OYSTER COUCH BLUES

Barbara Paturick

First Printing 1984

ISBN 0-939602-02-4

Library of Congress Number: 84-072698

Design and Layout by Robin Tewes

Published by Blue Star Press
        163 Joralemon St., Suite 1144
        Brooklyn, N.Y. 11201

 Produced at The Print Center, Inc., Box 1050, Brooklyn, N.Y.,
11202, a non-profit printing facility for literary and arts-related
publications. Funded by The New York State Council on the
Arts and the National Endowment for the Arts.

For Rachel Mia

TABLE OF CONTENTS

Notes From New York City

Ramona a/k/a Mimi

O.K. California

NOTES FROM NEW YORK CITY

FLATBUSH

The folks around here hate
Black People.
(They're really terrified of them.)
They don't understand pierced noses
or high ass.

This urban rot box
sifting people separately then
lumping them together
for the kill.

KELOIDS

Black skin
how it heals
so sadly.

The iron burnt Mary Cole-
man's arm
and her burden became
heavier to bear.

In a fight once
Bonda stabbed Dennis
with an ice pick.
His leg smiled pink for years.
"This is where Bonda stabbed me."

THE HUMANITIES

He brings Salsa to college
his heart beating to the tune of the forest,
his Chemistry booked by his love light.

When he enters the classroom
the teacher grimaces
something about the "proficiency exam".
The music dies down
spirit suppressed inside the magic
FM box.

TWO SIDES OF A COIN

Last night Rachel woke up
coughing.
She called me to her room
MOMMY MOMMY
COUGHING COUGHING COUGHING
Finally she spit up.
Her spit came elastic milky
one continuous fluid
in my hair, in my arms.
We kissed. I hugged her
You're O.K You're O.K.
I cleaned her up
changed the sheets
tucked her in
warmed her
"Tomorrow you'll give up the bottle?"

This morning trotting down
gray subway stares
a large pool of spit & vomit.
I wonder did this pool
come from this man
at the same time
that Rachel
spit into my arms?
Two people spitting
stereophonic
one into her mother's breast
the other wretching cold
on winter street face pavement
tears.
"I'll give up the bottle."
"I'll give up the bottle."

LOVESONG

Perfect little cloves
kissing each other sheathed
in parchment.
Said to do away with headaches
and improve circulation.
An ancient vegetable
cousin to the onion.
THE HELL WITH BAD BREATH
I LOVE IT!

Earlier in my life I couldn't stand it.
Now I can feel its effect in my body
making my blood bristle, alert.
Who knows what other changes it
has wrought in me?
Lately I think about traveling
to Italy alot.

Three ways I enjoy Garlic that I never
would've dreamed possible before:
1. Sauteed with spinach or escarole
2. In a scungilli salad (a topic suitable
    for doctoral dissertation)
3. Tucked behind the ear lobes for night
    magic

MADONNA FORKPITCHING IN PLAIN SIGHT
('I'm jes mindin the child')

The two year old
with forty eyes,
eyes all over the
outside of his body,
each patch of skin an
        eye,
Embarrassed.

He knew I knew
He cried out
Forty eyes.

Brown as limpid mud pools
Brown as the inside of all our
        souls
Brown on the way to heaven
Brown with high I.Q.'s & atom bombs
        (nuclear fishin')

He knew I knew
he was being abused
pert cap on his head
poking witch fingers
debauching his face.

BIG DEVIL GIANT WITCH
    UNMIND
    UNMIND
    UNMIND THAT CHILD!

14

DOLORES #1

Usually I wear dungarees
but I was going through a thing
thirty-one's were too big &
thirty's made me feel
like whipped cream in a corset.
The denin itched and cut
my crotch and
so I had no choice.
I put on these forest green
corduroy pants. Very fashion
able. They had stove pipe legs and
fit my tushy like a ski slope.
You could see my body sexing above
the sidewalk.

I walked past Dolores and she
was so impressed.

She said, "You know Bar-Bar-a you
could be poleece woman".

15

IN THE PLAYGROUND — BROOKLYN, U.S.A.

The boys smoke pot &
play ball.
They've got their bicycles
& their muscles in their thighs
OH MY!
And arms like hardened honey so
the basketball it twirls & bounces
bounces
       ounces.

Some of them look like Jesus
some like
Huck Finn
But none of them look like
Jack Paar.

THE BEGINNING OF CAPITALISM

I guess it hadn't taken hold yet,
the profit motive still young and confused
because beside my towering duplex
complex/plex/plex
(with escalating rents)
is a gray shingle house with a
real porch.
There's a bird house in the yard
and white flowering pear tree
blossoms gracing a lovely
square plot of land
filled with scattered daffodils
and bushes, maples and an attic.

The lady of this Brooklyn Manor
wears white spun hair
& pants
feeds birds her tip top bread ends
and cavorts with
her dear rotund mate
of reddened face
parking their falcon
in a decayed yet charming garage.

Some ancestor of the current
landlord gave this charming once
young couple a 99 yr. lease
and a rent of $80.

Since then the reins of
capitalism pull hard
on such idealistic crap
and these two souls
have been the victims
of endless attempts at their
eviction.

Two fires in their yard.
The tearing down of their gray
fence like braces off the teeth.
Now garbage mingles freely
with the fallen pears
and men pause there to piss
feeling welcome.
The lord and lady much too slow
of gait to bother.

(The new young landlord once wanted
this large home for himself,
but legality forbade it.
Ah Justice!
and now he lives
in Town Town Village)

And these old two with
49 yrs. left
shuffle slowly
feed the birds
feel indignant no doubt.
Not budging they.

So no one makes a profit on this deal.
Except the 2 old people
with their stable
rent and land.
A modest Brooklyn street
with Blimpies submarines
on the clothesline
and dacron french fries on the roof.
Big Daddy's Burger King Big
Mac Wrappers. daffodils.

Their Irish Son
comes from Jersey one
Sunday a month
to clean the refuse
                    refuse
                            refuse.

BLOODBATH

I just walked into the kitchen
where incidentally I'm defrosting
a wad of chopmeat.
The blood is dripping onto
the kitchen counter through
the plastic bag.
I know I should put the bag
with the dripping blood
in a dish.
(I'll never forget the time we lived
with steak blood dried & old beneath
the fruit bin.)
The smell.
The smell drove us mad
with embarrassment
(a dead lady with her period?)
fear
(a crushed and severed mouse?)
and anger
(is this fuckin place haunted or what?)
so, I definitely thought that
I should put that bloody speckled bag
in something.
And the last thing to catch my eye
as I walked out of the kitchen
was a large & milky plastic funnel.
So maybe that's the answer.
I should defrost my chopmeat
in a funnel.

NEW YORK MORNING

The IRT broke
I drive my husband to work
Wall Street a sea of inanity
scarves, cold noses
no posies.

My husband wears his baseball cap
and wants to quit his job.
"No writer would do this."

I feel sad
old yellow Monza with California plates
inching down Broad Street
Salvation Army corners us with bells and savings
but no help.

A young man runs alongside the traffic
pretending to be a car.
He has a horn and blinker and a pretty stubborn
clutch
that only he can see.

He gets a flat
What a blowout!
Tries to flag down motorists for help
but his legs arent pretty enough.

FIFTH FLOOR WALKUP

Young colt, Bert
I knew you in the East Village
our bodies so elastic,
gathered to what seems.

Today I saw a picture in
a child psychology book
& it was you . . .
young shining eyes, not sure
bones put together
by the MichaelAngelo of Gods.

You were my art piece,
flawless.
(You cried easily but quiet)

I felt your pain again today,
years later.

Page 176 in the Parent Book,
a Holistic Program for Raising the
Emotionally Mature Child.

A curiosity how you got there.

RENT INCREASE

The moon is very high tonight
and full
I could be on a mountaintop
but I'm on the 5th floor
with bars on my window.
The tree outside my window
is bright yellow
I walk along its shoreline
with my eyes for hours every day.
The tree is the reason I let
the landlord raise my rent.

THE BOY IN THE UNDERSHIRT

We were eating Chinese food
    or was it tuna fish?
We had traveled a long way
    to see Billy the Kid
and afterward we stopped for
Chinese Tuna Fish.
It was cold out,
stinging
and we were relieved to be
inside the little Mandarin
luncheonette.

I bit into my chow mein
holding it between two hands
and peered out the burglar
proof window.
At the moment we were happy
and not talking.

Across the street
on the top story
of a squat two story
Brooklyn hut
a boy in a timeless t-shirt,
a t-shirt for the entire universe,
paused in front of his window
and our eyes caught,
hooked.
He was muscular and
shiny
dark with blue
underneath his skin,
combing his hair upward
like a Cadillac fin.
He had earth trousers on
creased and
unamerican.

I smiled at you over a
pineapple coke
and wanted to tell you
what I'd seen.
But the boy in the timeless
t-shirt
was just a flicker,
a fantasy,
historic repitition
and I didn't feel like
making him reel.

HEAVY RAINS IN NEW YORK CITY

Flooding to the subway
Turnstiles
Turnstiles
Process Me
Always a rush
a high through
the turnstiles.
I love the fuckin turnstiles
Man & Machine in perfect synchronization
Token in the slot
click turn
rhythmic

& then the guy with his little bucket
comes and gets our tokens
counts em
gives em to the guy in the booth who
SELLS EM BACK TO US
full circle
The turnstile as mandala
The subway as Nirvana
Roaring through dark tunnels
Subterranean pop
corn on 14th street
People talking yelling to themselves
about their raw deal
while others look away
at others.

The day the rain was deep
all our soles made imprints
on the subway car floor
patterns more diverse than
sets of stars
designs more intricate than filigree
mosaic as telling as
the rings inside a tree.

The souls made patterns
    with their mud
Keds and   Earth Shoes
all of us negative heels
Shufflin
Shufflin
Shufflin
            to work.

A NEW LOOK AT THINGS

And my love, my wonder
Who thinks that water on her hair
makes it grow.
who loves to cook and paint at three
who makes me an imaginary sundae
with roast beef potatoes whipped cream &
a cherry,
you buffer my adult pain
forcing me
to consider the moon anew
and pigeons like they're peacocks.

TO THE YOUNG ART STUDENT

I OLD LADY
ME. I see you on the train
to Astor Place.
You young part of me
you wisps of hair
on face on face
lift hands
to grip
your Boston Bag
containing sketch
pad softly on athletic shoes
shows friend his drawing
dark hair falling
with a purpose a
cross dark eyes
embank high nose
who knows
intensive horsehoe mouth
for mutual help in breathing.

You my brother
brain sprouts brows diversely
drawing drawing.

I know your cousins &
how they think of you;
yet kindness peeling beneath
the ink, the ink, the autos
& Sheridan Square.

STILL LIFE

I found some baby pictures of me.
THAT'S NOT ME!!!
THAT'S NOT ME!!!

I study them real close.
I'm a victim
a poor and helpless victim.
I look for the clues, the connection
but I'm just another baby,
Am I just another person?
Part of the toll that each generation
takes on its clockwork life?

I'm strapped into a big carriage on
46th Street. I'm real big.
A BIG BABY!

I look silly in my dress and bald big
head.
My mother is just a young girl.
She has lipstick on and
I seem to mean alot to her,
but still,
my mother is just a young girl.

30

EARTH AND FEATHERS

There's alot of work
like deveining shrimp
and slimy chores
scrubbing   washing
        WOOSHING
water seems to play a big part.
in circular motions
the laundry room
and trickling over my skin
dish caress.

You work hard at your fun when
                you're a family.
After a day of movies
frozen milky ways bus rides bathrooms
and corkscrew conversation
you really gotta come home and
not kick off your shoes
not put on your favorite blues
BUT GIVE THE KID A BATH
        with her pissing doll and sponges.

Oh my beauty in the bath!
skinned ivory tomato,
singing rippling
"I hate the smell of Ajox mommy"
The hair wash, the terry robe and on
to changing rubber sheets
in clapboard rooms with
ripped yet hopeful jungle paper.

31

It's a lot of work
to have a little fun with a family
not like any abandonment I've
known before.
Rather a physical
earth and feathers
sweating under the tits
kind of joy.

Sometimes we all three kiss
mustache bristling on
bee stung lips
and mine so grateful, so grateful.

My daughter slips her hand in mine
walking up the street
going off to sleep
hugging chimp she blows spit
bubbles and drips yogurt down her chin.
And I have to get the paper towels.
The Bounty. It's really mine to have.

SEX APPEAL

The pedestrians on Park Avenue
            were shocked
to see a full grown man
in shorts & high heeled shoes
a sexual miscalculation
with lipstick curly
hair & smooth duck skin.

The man in the halter top
fluttered his eyelids
hiked up no tits
& clogged his way to Grand Central.

He knew the workmen
really saw him as bait.
It made things awful hard
for all of them.

THE LAST THREE DAYS

I struggled through the last three days
tearing holes in Wednesday's
                    pants leg
my teeth clenched   salivating
from my eye pockets
ending with a swollen gland.

I rose, I fell
I rode my nervous energy
creating new t-shirts, new ideas
for poems & stories
starting businesses,
cleaning the community,
reorganizing, reorganizing
applying to art school
dejected dejected
adopting children
all in these three days.

I glanced out the window
on night the third
the Moon FULL & TUGGING
(my genetics straining)
Even a drink won't help
my side hurts too much.

I flow with this anxiety
in the sense that I don't
see anyone
about it
and when I see myself
I'm not ashamed.

BROWN LEATHER

I heard that when they stick
a pin into a certain part
of your brain
your memory is activated
with startling accuracy
and I suppose sadness.

There must be a permanent pin
in that part of my brain
because I don't just live
I RELIVE for every moment
    of living.

Today on the subway
a brown leather jacket worn
& BANG
I see an old friend's leather
jacket.
I SMELL IT.
I feel him brown leather bagging me.

I remember being a little girl.
I wish my mother were riding
on this subway with me
her fat arms and her vaccination
cushioning the prick of this
pin.

BLIZZARD '78

I spent the day indoors
with you fair childe,
the snow aswirl outside
making travelers thick as pudding.

It must be God.

You blindfold me
and make me guess at objects
thrust into my hand.
A cradle? Snoopy? Pine cones?
My sense of touch renewed.
I feel each side of each object
and guess and guess and guess.

You wash your nightgown, tights and scarf
and hang them to dry above the bath.
Later at night, while submerged in bathwater,
I see from down below
your fluffy rags set out to dry
with soap caked deep in their folds.

Trying to clean up I trip on your
dolly's tea set
and fumble over the flag you made
wih fringes and a kite tail.

At 9:00 P.M. we visit a moving neighbor
to say goodbye.
It isn't until we sit around her kitchen table,
you in "feety" pajamas,
that I see how beautiful you are
your golden hair swept sideways
half skirting your right eye.
Your pale skin and dark brown eyes
and fluid movements
"curiouser and curiouser".
You try at five to understand the funereal talk
and the rose smatterered wallpaper
as you feed your plastic Patty
with a minute nursing bottle.

When Irene offers you all her M&Ms and Hershey Candy
you poise above each dish
and smear your face with chocolate,
young tribal maid, forever Halloween.

As I crawled into my bed tonight
my toes hit scissors
my hands pulled up around my breast
a quilt made hard with drops of Elmer's Glue.
Stubby crayons stuffed behind my pillowcase
as I prepare to sleep.

Closed behind the eyelids of the night
my mind loosens.
I see the wrinkle in your upper cheek
extend from the contagion of your smile.

It must be God.

FEMALE FORM

When your arms encircle me
nude
my form is defined.
My breasts press into your bare chest
your hand travels my hips my ass
the curving snake — my waist.

During the day I might be walking around
formless with a shopping cart,
but when we slip into bed
flesh pressing flesh
I become a lotus flower
apple core
perfectly shaped for the action.

NO RMS NO VU

On a block forgotten by dignity
On a block punctuated by dog feces
      & garbage
Alongside a wall of peeling rock
      posters
lies a single step.
A 9x12 step
with an arch overhead
and tiny walls on either side
and this she calls her home.

There are no photos of dead lovers or children
hanging by the hearth
and no religious candles burning.
No potholders
No samplers extolling the virtue
of living on a step.

She has a variety of bags
filled with the nonsense that
won't meet her needs.
Her hair is matted & old
several colors and
itchy, itchy, itchy.

I pass her everyday and wince.
She sits in a puddle and never
dares
to look me in the eye
although I try, I try.

Her skin is coated with a thin layer
of purple fungus
Her tongue has fur on its edges
Does she speak?
No. She's still looking for her teeth
her bones, her heart that cracked
her brain that didn't pull her through.

Day after day
she's there
relaxing on her Barca Lounger
on a wet step in icy New York City
with a bottle of Old Mr. Boston Lemon Flavored Gin.

One day I pass by and
she's not there.
And then another
and another.
Blotted out like too much messy lipstick
on tissues, bloated
paper furniture gone
formica dining set
chandelier
princess phone
gone on the wet step.
Not even a fossil or
a spec remains
of the lady whose heart
was crushed by a cruising
Mac Truck on a joyless ride
called commerce,
New York City.

CROSSING FLATBUSH AVENUE

The light changed
WALK
DON'T WALK
DO AS I SAY.
People started to cross.
The rules are clear enough.
But there was a driver
who just wasn't thinking
social conscience at that time.
He was thinking "dare me"
and he raced through the light
nearly mowing us
nerf pedestrians down.
Some Black people, an old lady
with them, she looked like
nosy Mrs. Brown
spoke about the incident:
"Man I thought the light had changed"
Mrs. Brown, wearing the hat
I made for Mary Nichols in millinery shop
said, "Yeah but that fool don't know it."
They were coming at me, The Browns
and I continued crossing the street.
I felt really good and in
love and glad to be in New York

RAMONA a/k/a MIMI

Vincent Van Gogh before his death to his brother Theo . . .

La tristesse durera toujours.
The sadness will always remain.

ROSH HASHANAH – 1976

Mimi loved the Tayglich
but she's dead.

She called it "the mountain"
but she's dead.

God wrote in his book on Yom Kipur
DIE MIMI DIE
and she did.

IN THE PAST TENSE

After her breakdown
she was confined in
Hillside Hospital,
"adolescent pavillion".
The doctor asked her
after 40 sessions of no talk
"Well what kind of music do you like?"

"Nina Simone. . . ."
The first exchange between them.

Four days later
she shot shaving cream into
his office
but noticed he was listening
to Nina sing "Oh Lord Please Don't Let
Me Be Misunderstood"
with that bitch the social worker.

After a year of 800 mg. of thorazine
and stitching three stuffed pillows a day,
a medical journal in a vacant
waiting room
informed her that
"drug therapy was becoming stylistically passe."

Her bone marrow drained
into her depression.
She made no note,
but closed the book.

MYCLONIC JERK AND OFF INTO THE HINTERLANDS

Drifting, floating on the bed
Drifting off to you
MIMI?
All sorts of images in
der my head.

Myclonic jerk
down a flight of
stares. . . . .
It's scary to die
when living is what you
do every day.
That old living habit
kind of gets you hooked,
I never knew much else
from pablum on
and on and on.
How did you know the
alternative so well?
Suicidal with such assurance!
Hats off to you as I drift by.
Myclonic jerk down a
flight.

MOBSTER BISQUE

Even though she read Steinbeck
     & Dostoevsky &
hummed Of Human Bondage
she had to be a barmaid
        or a clerk.

She had to clerk while her
whole body a heart
her brain a heart
her feet, her tears
a heart.

She drank her liquor
straight
& mostly loved & tried to
squeeze it
out of men
who censured her soul for
sprouting her womanly body.

In the center —
fold in two cups of flower
pinch of salt
(a tear will do)
& one cup softened pan juice.
Blend an hour
pour forever.

Watch it drip outside the mold.
NO LUCK.

TO BOB SARGENT

I read propped up a
layman's medical dictionary.
Always fun for the neurotic
a time of joy and figuration
translating simple aches and pains
into larger more important things.

At the end of the book —
a guide to modern first aid.
I study the current acceptable
method of artificial respiration.
Mouth-to-mouth is in,
with a footnote for those of
squeamish nature
(*breathe into a conical hanky and then
transfer to patients mouth)

Admittedly somewhat less effective.

I think of you, Bob Sargent
a man I hardly ever knew
my next door neighbor
so short a time,
I think of you unshaven
despairing
when your candidate McGovern lost the race.

I think of your lovely wife Leah
and the cordialities, the almost teas
and near friendship that passed
between our apartmentalized lives
and in a startling picture image
I see you artificially respirating
(*without a conical hanky)
the dying blue gray face of my
dear sister.
Did you wipe her inside mouth of mucus
like the book advised?

"A non-breathing person never bites."

I think of you, Bob Sargent
and see you knealing hopeless
over her young corpse,
my own true love,
while I dream-knowing walked
on Brighton Beach.

You, waiting for the emergency squad
"they'll do it!"
You, who share a love for Dickens with my
Bob, yet unbeknownst.

You knowing what it means to
try to save a life
without ever having known
its delicacy
its special language
movements
feisty spirit
always confined, unable to alight
until you leaned on top of her
to breathe your body's breath
your life's handle
into her rejecting heart.
Then did she fly away
for good.

I spoke to Leah after the death.
She told me you two had to get away.
I never spoke to you at all.
But now in my way

choked as ever
(no scar has formed but still
an open wound)

I speak to you with thanks for earnest trying.
Somehow similar
all   our paths crossed curious
never to cross again.

2

Mimi: her young body
meditteranean hair
(what difference all the yogurt she ate?)
She dies   she dies
unhappiness & booze
a screamer in the library
  black winged dove
bombing her every depression
contemplating her thick eyebrows
Joan Crawford?
dark eyes
an overlapping tooth
thank god she never got
that nose job.
the casket closed—did they remove her coil?
a face with character
what matter now?
maybe you thought
'But I just heard her
Nina Simone
through thin skinned walls'
It skipped
It skipped
the beat to stop
her heart.

You must've thought as you labored,
slapped and huffed in fear
SHIT DAMN IT
JESUS CHRIST!
So young my god
so young.

52

RACHEL AGAIN

Haunted, always thinking
of the MIMI in you
the scales of my dead sister shed
reveal a chubby satin you.

> Spirutually this may or
> may not be true
> Practically
> and on this earth
> you left my dear sweet MIMI
>   behind
> you maybe kept her eyelashes
> and of course her dramatics
> her humility
> her need for me to love her.

You were conceived in the same corner
minute area of the world in which
she lost her life.
Only a month to pass between
your two existences.
You never knew her personally
although the thoughts of her gray ghost
shook my womb with sorrow
while you prepared your world debut.

My love . . .
so much to be said of my dead sister,
you her namesake,
but already my eyes are readying for the
rain.
My heart cracks,
the endless gorge of sorrow
always at my beck and call.

THE LAST STANZA

Time she goes too fast
flying past my doorstep
and my bra.
Death I draw no closer to you
being of you
I know you'll come whenever you please.
SURPRISE!!!
The horns will blow
I'll lose my mind
my precious thoughts and reasonings.

I can let go of my body.
I have no desire to preserve
its crumbling prison cells,
but, mind come with me!
Come with me on the long ride
through dark familiar tunnels
sunlit fields of buttercups
undulating to the shore.
Waves crash
I'm drawn upon your beach, death,
lying still
guessing at half truths
yanking curtains back to find no view.

I need my thoughts to
build others
to comfort me
to swathe my broken heart
in a psychology.

ROBERTO CLEMENTE

Roberto Clemente
dead inning plane crash.
His wife and children
puzzle
peace.
A stadium-his name-to-come.

Ramona Paturick
dead-on-her vial.
Her sister
Her sister
remembers holding her hand to sleep
writes poems for her name
knows sooner that death is to be.

She spoke a different language
and he
Roberto Clemente
Ramona Paturick
souls released
young and smattered
in the same space and
climb.

AUTOPSY '72

They nabbed you, sweet and fragile bird.
Once they caged you in the
Women's House of Detention
now torn down and
you torn down
and ripped apart in City Morgue,
those awful saws
defiled you into triangles . . .

In City Morgue with toe tags
and fingernails flung from fleshy tips
"She looks much older than her age."
Sure she does, you fools. She's dead.

They nabbed you young and breathful
at Kennedy Airport and ripped
your coat apart. "What's this?"
They examined you vaginally and threw you
sweet and fragile bird
into a cell with three bull-dykes
"Hey baby got a smoke?"

Those cries each time they locked you up!
Hospitals, schools, jails . . .
and then to City Morgue at twenty-two
"possible strangulation"
your black hair falling,
felled
around your lovely shoulders,
your boyish hips gone slack,
All your sexuality on a tray

oh sweet and fragile bird.

They nabbed you at Johnnies Lounge
in leotard and girly tights, Tortilla
Flat on the bar.

SINCE YOU HAVEN'T CALLED

The New York Life, Ramona
So Close to death.
did I hear you laugh?
Floating unencased
free sausage meat,
I push the turnstile
quickly, quickly
while my head flashes
to bars
to bars and drinks
with you.
A real down person you
were.
You were. You were?
Down & loose &
anarchic
by nature.

THANKSGIVING 1970 — A MESSAGE FOR RAMONA

Your ex-boyfriend rang my bell today
with all his drink & violence
and two enjellied turkey rolls
to wish you via me
"A Happy Thanksgiving."

Two turkey rolls
I carried sullenly
from the lobby to my door
in their foil and cardboard
containers and
plunked them on my table.

You draw in blood, Ramona,
missing such a schizoid love.
The two of you like crazy hawks
circling the sky
his eyes a chunk of that.
You peck at your dissipated livers
heartbeat
and the idea of an ocean breeze
to the rescue.

"SEX IS OUT, DEATH IS IN"
N.Y. Times Book Review

The symbol of the hereafter
makes the death knell a wafer.
I accept it without apprehension,
my mouth hung slack.

This morning I awaken from a dream
(At least I know the quality of those)
And it is you I think of,

Dead Sister
Dead Sister
Dead Sister

The thought of your death is repulsive,
too painful, too blinding
for morning.

Dead sister,
who slept with me in sisterhood
who grew amongst my girlhood
with soft brown velvet eyes
and pick-up sticks and stories.

I know about dreams and how I dream them,
but I don't know about where you've gone.

Dead sister, with the self of pain-ridden soul
and life with the quality
of dreams.

A QUIRKY REACTION

Dead Squirrels
Dead Dogs
Dead Raccoons on the road.

I swerve to avoid
a multiple murder.
Urge suctions from my loin.
Dead Dogs
down the birth canal.
All animal life
squashed between my legs.

HANDOUTS FROM THE DEAD

MIMI
we always wished for
power
in high places and
well you're up there
flying above Brighton
and the 69 cent shops
How bout it?
Pull some strings on
your celestial harp.
Make my life jazz together
the way yours never did.
You know.
Nobody knows as well as you
or Marilyn Monroe
or of course the living me
how senseless blue
that life can be.
So
how bout it?
Come on.
I can't be an accountant
or a palamino
not this time.

My husband tried to work
on Wall Street
but his tie got caught
in his lower lip and
his mustache walrused
the moon.
So
I beseech thee
oh living angel
up high
lay something on us
a means
in America
a means
for two poets
to afford some ski ball
and a car
and a free pass
beyond the questions
"Have you tried teaching out-a-state?"
"How about Civil Service in Honduras?"
MIMI
you know that
speedwriting only gets you
a quicker obit.
Clams on the half shell & margueritas
take money to get.

THE CEMETERY

On the way to your grave
for the first time.
I buy wine so you can get high
and flowers for your kitchen table.

At the florist shop
the salesman says,
"Would you like to enclose a card?"
I laugh. You ghost.
How about Happy Halloween?

April 6 or so, 1976

My dream last night:

Mimi limp and bony at the foot of my bed. Lying down.
Oh Mimi, really physically you. I, propped up on pillows,
Grandma Beckie next to me. Already dead. Mimi sweating and
dying, dead. In the living room my mother and father watching
T.V. Mimi dies. I wait patiently. Mimi is ressurected. Grandma
Beckie says "Don't worry this is as it should be." Mimi and I
converse. She asks where she is. I tell her "You're dead." But I
can still touch her and hold her. My love. Long hair. She says
she lost her New York State mind. I tell her she'll be reincar-
nated, that's the way it happens. She looks at me and gives
me her wry Mimi-laugh. That's what you think is in her eyes.

My father comes in perplexed. "Who's talking, what's going
on?" I scream at him and push him away — back to the *living
room.* "GODDAMNIT CAN'T I HAVE ANY PRIVACY
AROUND HERE?" Beckie says "Get rid of him."

Mimi has to make. I take her to the toilet. She's limping
next to me hanging on to me frail sweaty. My dear. So skinny
and limp. She begins to urinate. I have to hold her on the
toilet. She's like a heap of soft things. She slides a little
bit off the toilet and some of the piss goes on the floor. She
gets real upset — angry at me for letting her make on the
floor – and upset at her own inabilities. I hug her, comfort
her. "Don't worry. I'll clean you up. I'll put powder on you and
make you all clean." My love.

ALTER EGO?

Push the mourning out of my head
Deal with the aftermath,
my life.

The cards are on the table
I can't KEEP crying.
Rachel's playmate will be here
at 2.
The whoops, the yells, the affirmations,
their lives.

The Queen of Hearts
one of her faces in the grave
the other,
my life.

THE PURSUIT OF HAPPINESS

Tonight I can only think of Mimi.
How much I want to hold her
cuddly dear
and kiss her quirks.

She's dead.
She's dead
WHAT'S THAT?

the line, the boundary
free speech
democracy
won't help me cross.

SUNDAY AUGUST 29, 1976

How are my dreams connected to my waking life?
I dream about bathing a baby in a tiny sink.
The next day I *see* that sink in a doctor's
office. I dream about putting spare ribs on a
shelf.

I symbolize my feelings. I intuit what may happen
to me or has happened in too distant a past. Every
night I go to sleep expecting. I expect my dreams to
answer me, lead me where in waking life the thick
walls of reality don't allow me to go.

IT'S TRICKY TO THINK OF SOMEONE YOU LOVE AS DEAD

Even though you died, Ramona,
I see you around sometimes.
The other day outside the CO-OP Supermarket
I saw you driving a van.
It was you, all right.

Dead people are like that, you know.
They can die in New York
and show up for some shopping
in California.

BURIAL IN FARMINGDALE

A rip off
with a fake rabbi
and a burial in Long Island.
The antithesis of your death
plans.
There was no sprinkling
of your spirit over crashing
waves.
No people in dramatic capes and hats
throwing single flowers in a field
but all of us on Amsterdam Avenue
your parents being Jewish
but without affiliation
knew no other way.

Your friends were there
your lover was forbidden
besides he had no pants.

The rabbi said some
slanderous things &
didn't give a shit.
Charles was nervous
Roz was on her way to
Albuquerque
Joanne just looked
confused.
Your coffin shut &
all your shitty aunts
were there.
NOBODY KNEW YOU!
just another casualty.

It made me sick
your funeral
for months.
Dad said Kaddish
at your grave

You didn't even know
what that was.
I kept hoping months
thereafter
that you weren't trapped
inside that tomb.
Your fear of being jailed
MY GOD
you said, "I won't be buried
with those jerks in Farmingdale"

On my first visit to your grave
there was a deep hole
where your hand spent its time
clawing out, but the plot had truly
thickened.

BOTH WAYS

What is this remembrance, MIMI?
I can talk of you
but how I miss the realness of your flesh.
The hugs you gave me
the crooked smile.

You were a spirit while alive
tinkerbelling across the streets of New York.

I was blessed to know your love.

O.K. CALIFORNIA

REUBENS WOMAN

I feel more athletic, Sagittarian
when my inner thighs are taut
but tonight I delight
I let flow loosely my flesh
and succumb to the blatant fact
that I AM A REUBENS WOMAN.

My belly has grown round
my thighs are padded at the top
my tush a few degrees more
to the compliment of gravity.
I have a beauty mark right above
my outy belly button
and tonight it sits as if
on the bottom of a gently sloping
hill.

There is a comfort
  a less aggressive sexuality
to the lookof it.
A filled out belly pucker
fuck to it.

I sense lush gardens as the
backdrop to my form
resting on a cool rock
I gain the respect of time.

BEFORE THE BIRTH OF MY SON

He moves!
His fists within me
stretching to thin parchment
the walls of his encasement.
He moves!
Demanding meat
to swell his head, grow hard his limbs
solidify his shield
for future conquests.
I feel him strain and
burst with the call of his own life
his mission apparent but never stated.

I sit and study Pope and Dryden
and am urged by his fetal pushes.
Urged to the kitchen for meat
and cheese and eggs and fish
Ingesting all at intervals
only for his rising, his ascent.

HE MOVES!
He punches, maybe considers a thought,
He moves inside his mother
as his father danced within her walls before.

JUNE

The young woman, June
cast out of the womb
like garbage from the back of a truck.

Cast out to be handled
and poked by sad branding irons
each orifice braised, searing.

Cast out from New York to New Mexico to
                California
Knocked up, knocked down
to bear her son
                his handsomeness.

Years of public assistance
with no help at all.

The young woman, June
cast out in Berkeley
hugged by a church
of feelingless mutes
                Hester Prinnized
and smacked upon the stone.
She's cold and so hungry,
the young woman, June.

Years of public assistance
with no help at all.

The poverty of no love, the corporeal
                starving
society's fault
to quake the thoughts, the desires
of the young woman, June.

77

She goes by with stolen shoes
and half-sewn dresses
hemmed by dark imaginings
and no friends. All too afraid
of THE MADWOMAN JUNE.

"Planes trail me by day,
by night I am raped,
my writings ransacked
by drug-laden creatures
who know,
THEY KNOW
that I can read their minds
and the minds of disc jockeys
who know when I masturbate
who are onto my secret —
THAT I AM WRITING ALL THE CURRENT ROCK
    AND ROLL".

The young woman, June
"Houses ablaze around me,
they're all on to my powers and
want to destroy me."
suffers alone
on Milvia Street
old ropes round her neck
and common words' meanings elude her.

"I furnished my whole apartment from
                a free-box,"
She is so pleased.
The vice-like plants and macrame,
the old Avon-calling castaways
strangle her caller
with pity.

Years of public asssistance
with no help at all.

Sometimes to see her!
the huge body heaving
the knowledge of her parent's abuse
on her gait,
her blonde hair more girlish
than sugar and spice. . . .

The young woman, June
on the brink
being followed and monitored
her dutiful son at the rear
like soft foldable cotton shirts.
Her fear yet pursuit of the sexual nightmare.

I want to cry, but it means nothing.
Her telepathy won't pay her rent
or teach her how to cook.
Alone out there, I can't help.
I've been there before
as witness and traveller
sucked through the whole of
                    madness.

I cry, but it means nothing
in the face of my fear
and inconsequence.
You know, she's had

Years of public assistance
with no help at all.

TO A FRAMED PICTURE

We are not organized
none of the furniture's right.
The style is off,
quite Irish.
The dash is slapped
between the I's of our
writing, our books, our ideas.

In a fit of homeyness
In a fit of desire to decorate
I buy a gilded picture frame at
the local 5 & 10.
It is plastic, sprayed golden
yet a thing of artistic beauty to me.
You sent me for an egg poacher
and I return with a gilded picture frame.
"What's in the bag? I'm afraid to ask."

I spent an hour in our carton.
Our California carton.
Pluto . . The Berkeley Hills . . The Bay.
I fished out a profile of you,
the sun catching every singular red hair
in your dark Sicilian beard.
Your forehead of Kings,
Your forehead of past lives
as Roman Emporer and
Grecian Thinker.
The sad look you never completely conceal
with your wit.

I pushed that picture against the glass and
cardboard and the deep burgundy velvet backing
and let the little tongue of a stand lean
cool against the dresser.

There you are, my troy of gold,
my find.
What if you should die?
There you are on the dresser, looking off,
handsome and fat and
sure of yourself.

I feel the house is redone,
refurbished,
replenished with the star of your face.

FOR BOB

My dearest beautiful face
Full lips
Will the sports awaken you?

Mindballs rolling in their sockets
shades drawn.
Tufts of bristly hair
deliberate on your flesh
your flesh soft canvas on
the frame of your bones
your princely sensual bones.

I hear the faintest snore!
An inner gust,
the man inside you growls!
My woman cleaves to you
electric drawn.

My tired thinker
resting on your boulder forearms
the hands that could punch my teeth out
usually fondle my breasts
or crease and rustle pages in the night.

ODE TO JELLY

Down Aisle Five
Condiments Napkins Toothpicks &
Olives.
I become transfixed before the jellies.
I feel ecstatic, forcing my
giggle to smile.
POLANER SEEDLESS BLACBERRY JAM!!

Blackberry jam is my delight.
my mother never looked like Katharine Hepburn
nor did she make fresh blackberry jelly,
but somehow I feel she did.
I can smell it in the kitchen in the big steel pot.
I would pick the berries and put them into wooden buckets
then ma or Katharine Hepburn (when she wasn't making
chopped liver) would steam the beautiful berries
in her pressure cooker.

Voila! Hebrew Zion Jelly!

Once I did pick berries in the Catskills.
That was my heaven,
the fruit from the vine
earth blood on my fingers.
Delicate clusters of ooze
in thin raspberry skin.

We ate our blueberries or strawberries
with sour cream and
had pumpernickel bread and butter
on the side.
My brother would blenderize the
strawberries&creamtogether
(A base adulteration in my opinion)
The result being a liquified meal
light pink
a soup for toast and butter
to skinny dip in.

Elivira Madigan ate her berries dipped in sweet cream
with her lover.

There I was transfixed by the jellies
Happy. Excited.
Mint flavored apple jelly
Transparent on my tuna fish.
Welch's Grape
Passable with cream cheese.
My heart dips at the sight of
the Prune Butter.
the veritable filling of grandma dora's humintash
in a jar!
There's Five Fruit Jelly
A symphony!
Smear it on my chicken
lick it off my lamb
jellify my every meal
squeeze the blackberry stuff
in my omelets and over
my deaf smith peanut
butter resting on a ritz.

I ended up with the
POLANDER SEADLESS BLACKBERRY JAM
I wanted more but
I was on a diet and had to forego the
mint jelly, the prune butter,
the black cherry preserves.
My tuna would stand with
the cottage cheese alone.
Blah.

Next night
in a moment of jelly weakness
I slabbed the dark black ruby stuff
between two slices of Edam Cheese
and slipped into Jelly Nirvana.

LETTER TO A FRIEND WITH THE OYSTER COUCH BLUES

August 10, 1978

She paid $1800 for a velvet couch. She said she picked it out
herself and its color was smoke or oyster. She came home
and felt unhappy:

"There's one thing you may not know about an oyster couch,
and this may be the source of your unhappiness. It requires
constant care and feeding and have you given thought to
grooming? Does thrice daily sound too rigorous? I hear one
cannot let these things go or else one is inevitably stuck
with a useless, shopworn commodity capable of providing
only a place for sitting. Can you imagine? Well!!
I never. . . ."

BERKELEY MAILBOX

 I was thinking of giving up poetry
when walking to get my mail
I spied a blonde lady passing by.

I was arrested for an instant,
ripe peach that she was,
succulent,
giving the air a splendid niche
to hang around.

I got my mail as she passed by.
(There was no lightning struck
acceptance of my work.)

but she stayed in my mind,
ripe peach that she was,
and succulent,
she made me smile.

I knew I couldn't give up poetry
because of the way I saw her.

THE PLANT LIFE or
Mixed Feelings about Sunlight and Clorophyll

Crying to the coleus of my heart
hanging there like a plant too big for its pot.

I grab on to life.
I don't want the trellis of my body
to give way
Although my leaves and vines
grow tedious
with their clinging.

CLICK-CLACK:
The shudders of my mind
elipse your beauty, sister.

You, compelled to die young
Who had to leave me here to
see this strange and orange California,
to fight against the impulse to give in.

My days are filled with the usual, poetry and tears.
But, oh, this new found Berkeley
with the sky so inimitable
the trees at peace with no smog showing.

Oh Bay and Mountains
sandals, wheat germ
avacado loin of lemon tree earth
Where is your pastrami?
Hiding in the scorched grass of your hills?
Showing where your bayview eyes blink patio cafes
and Chinese tea rooms?

My mind sheds visions of the
tense wheel turning in New York.

THE CRICKETS IN BERKELEY

Before 9:15 P.M. I didn't hear a sound.
At 9:15 on the button
the crickets starting singing, heaving,
filling the air with their short-breathed
whistling
crickets crickets
occupying every inch of aero-space.

Are there crickets in the after-life?
Are there crickets on Broadway and 42nd Street?
Do crickets ever go out to dinner?

NO! Crickets are hopelessly compelled
to rub their legs together; their angst.
We like to say "the crickets are singing",
ignoring their unhappiness,
working the nightshift,
compelled.

SPUTNIK & SPICE

I remember Sputnik
  how cute it was,
  like Lassie,
The cartoon of its design
  how harmless and a-
  technological.
Traveling in space
for power? I don't know. . .

Yet my heart journeys with
Marco Polo & Columbus & their pals.
What is more worth seeking out
than mustard, coriander
chocolate and the like?

I'd mission to Mars
for coffee
or ginger or sage;
that which charms my
chicken, mouth waters
my duck or makes my
beets thump,
YES.

Maybe moon dust on my
lamb chops or Saturn's
red gasses curried in
my stew pot would make
Mariner 2 worth
the thyme.

THE SWEETNESS OF CRYING

I cry now at most everything
for all of it is touching.
News shows, birds feeding
on the berry bush,
actors reading lines too loudly.

A young Jewess came over to my house
her topaz eyes as round as any game court,
a nose suggesting regal missions.

Young lady, now of the twentieth century,
the twentieth-Synanon-follow-the-leader-century,
playing in my house
laughing about farts
and Charlie Brown,
your parents divorced
living in Marin County
soaking in a hot tub
instead of soaking the chicken,
koshering it.

I cry now at most everything
mothers who are college graduates
and talk of Bing Crosby
or hard drinking men.
The world becomes infinitely more beautiful
with its layers of pretension, shellac
over time-worn photos.

Yesterday my Japanese neighbor spoke
about her move to America;
"Could not communicate with anyone."
Her proficiency in English a source
of ardent pleasure now.
"Would be like frog at bottom of well
if never left Japan."
Masako, yes.
To strive and fall upon your face,
the Shavian spiral upward.
Patricia MacBride straining
her balletic leg
piercing space upon the stage.
Lincoln Center one long gasp,
a burst of applause from the tiers!
and tears and tears from me.

THE CASE AGAINST FEAR

I could snap again
or flip my wig
or simply go nuts.

I could swallow my tongue,
        petit mal,
but I wanna enjoy a cup of coffee
in the morning
with a smile on my face.

O.K., O.K.,
Enjoy a cup of coffee real tense.

TABLE FOR ONE

Making breakfast — a thrill.
Bacon, eggs & melted cheese on toast.
It's so nice to care for yourself.
I eat this meal alone.
A glory.
I made it just for me.
I brewed a whole fresh pot of coffee
for myself. I take a multi
vitamin after the whole shabang.
I even set my place.
I read about Robert Frost
throughout the meal.
The bacon crisp, the eggs a fluffy yellow.
My whole grain bread like cake.

I can remember when I drank
gin or wine for breakfast,
but these eggs, this poetry,
this new love
for the art inside me
cut loose my spirit more.
A subtler moment, an awareness more acute
sad/happy
I CARE ABOUT HOW I'M ALIVE.
I HAVE MUSIC IN MY SOUL,
the beat less furious

a simpler pace

a focus.

FOOD FOR THOUGHT

What is every day to the bird?
the bee?
The quick find or
the forage.

They skitter about the yard
darting squirrels
rabbits that know how to stand
taxidermy still.

Why is my sense of
defeat so grand?
I look for scraps that mean something.
The quick find or
the forage.

SALVE FOR MY HUSBAND'S WOUNDS

I called the publisher today
and when she got back on the phone
she said in hushed yet grated tones
"I'm afraid I have bad news. I'm terribly sorry."

Just like someone had died
Just like getting a positive
on a rabbit test
when you're sixteen and you don't want a baby.

"I'm afraid I have bad news. I'm terribly sorry."

Seven months of consideration.
"We have to decline . . .
the letter will explain. Mr. Zackheim
extends his apologies."

Seven months of thinking
what else could they decide after
all this time?

Seven months of planning our new life.

I hung the phone up and
cried. Short and hard.
I cried.
I can take it.
Give me more
Give me more.

I cried for your work
and its urgency
and our not knowing where to send it.

Reading Zukofsky and wanting Europe to embrace
your work
like stupid, facile America never could.
I cried for the countless rejections
and years slipping by
our young lives pained
by the windows of no possibilities.

THE HEART OF THE MATTER

They're having a fight in apartment 5.

"How could you study economics?"
"Zionism and Apartheid!!"
Screaming, Tension, Tempers Fly.

Our principles are our blood.
Without them our hearts
shrivel into petty organs
capable of only the ticking.

TRANSCENDENTAL MEDITATION

Shy Om Shy Om Shy Om
Here she comes Shy Om
I'm . . . Shy Om
that fuckin bastard if she opens
that door Shy Om Shy Om
Fry the eggplant or
bake it?
Shy Om Shy Om
here the fuck she comes
she has so much fucking nerve
Shy Om
that fucking middle class
broad
that self centered ass
Shy Om Shy Om
Shy Om Shy Om

"Whadya Want?
It's on the desk —
hey look fuck face
you can just move out"
Shy Om
"I'm Meditating!!"

THE BLONDE FROM CEDAR

I never saw the stately blonde from Cedar
off her skates.
She skated her young son to Montessori School
and skated her Schnauzer for his daily walk.
She skated to Kaleidoscope, a bookstore down the block,
and skated in.

Her six-foot frame remained
poly-urethaned on wheels.
Her daily chores, a folly.

One Saturday at Iceland, there she was.
This time on ice skates tooling, gliding,
blonde hair flying,
one too many wrinkle round her eyes.
Her thin body like the page of a book
turning against the drudgery of life.

On a day I least expected it
I saw the stately blonde of Vermont vintage
walking down the street!
I was shocked to see
she did not really know the art of walking,
like a wooden dragon in a Chinese gift shop
(with fragmented vertebrae)
she chopped along the sidewalk,
all, but not at once.

That day the blonde from Cedar
left her stately presence
hanging limply on the hook in her hallway.